LUCY LONG AGO

UNCOVERING the MYSTERY of WHERE WE CAME FROM

Catherine Thimmesh

Houghton Mifflin Books for Children
Houghton Mifflin Harcourt
Boston New York 2009

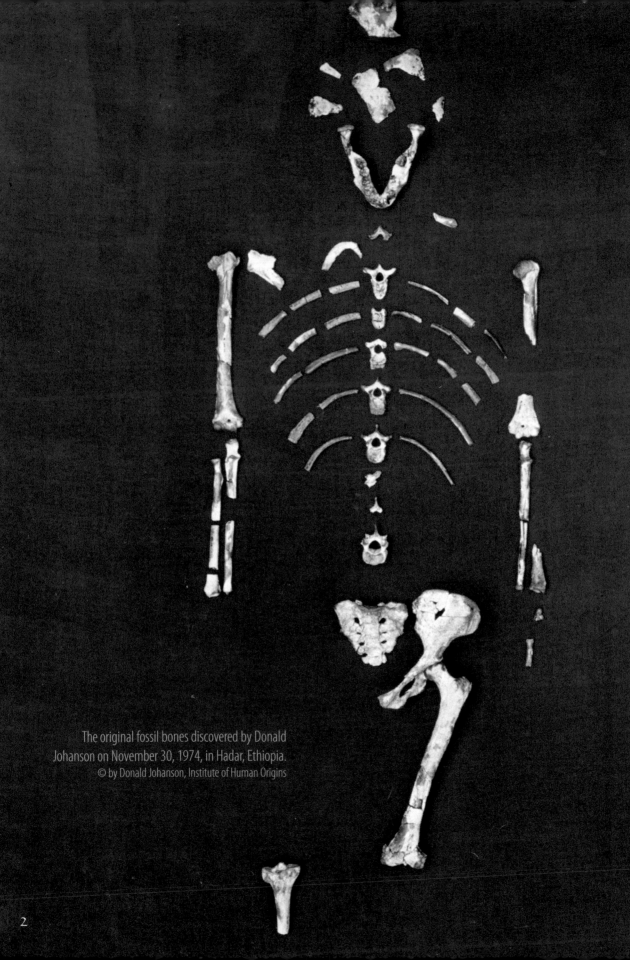

The original fossil bones discovered by Donald Johanson on November 30, 1974, in Hadar, Ethiopia.
© by Donald Johanson, Institute of Human Origins

IT

Long ago, it lived . . . even before it had a name. It climbed trees; it roamed the savannah on two legs; it munched on berries and grasses.

In its time, the dinosaurs had been extinct for more than sixty million years. A few million years would pass before modern humans would walk the earth that it now roamed upon.

One day though, it crumpled to the ground and lay in a heap. Unmoving.

Soon after, floodwaters churned. Sand and silt sloshed over it, providing a cozy burial blanket—tucking it quietly away from the rough-and-tumble of the outdoors. In time, that wet, sandy muck hardened, trapping its bones tight. A volcano erupted, ash rained down, settling on and sealing the rock. It lay snuggled in stone for more than three million years.

United States
of America

Ethiopia

Region
of Hadar

CHILD OR GROWNUP?

"Nothing quite like it had ever been discovered," explains paleoanthro-pologist Donald Johanson. "The camp was rocking with excitement. The first night we never went to bed at all. We talked and talked. There was a tape recorder in the camp, and a tape of the Beatles song 'Lucy in the Sky with Diamonds' went belting out into the night sky, and was played at full volume over and over again out of sheer exuberance."

Its resurrection began on a hot, sticky day in Hadar, Ethiopia, in November 1974. The scientist who stumbled upon it, who discovered that first bit of elbow jutting out of the sediment, was, in fact, searching for it. Had, in fact, traveled to the other side of the world hoping to find it. Or someone like it . . . he wasn't that picky. He was hunting hominids: skeleton bones of human ancestors.

Donald Johanson and a team of scientists were digging for bones, yes, but primarily they were detectives on a case. They were trying to solve one of the greatest mysteries of all time: *Where did we come from?* Each hominid fossil discovery was a clue; its analysis, a tiny piece of the giant jigsaw puzzle of human evolution.

So when Johanson, accompanied by his graduate student Tom Gray, happened upon an arm bone lying in a gully, he was understandably ecstatic. But when, a moment later, the two scientists realized they were looking at a partial skeleton of a single hominid individual—not just one bone—they leaped and hugged and howled for joy in the 110-degree heat (and then gingerly sidestepped and tiptoed so as not to crush the bones scattered on the ground, strewn at their feet).

"We've got it!" Tom Gray euphorically screamed when he and Johanson returned to the camp. "We've got The Whole Thing!"

The site in Hadar, Ethiopia, where scientists found the skeleton bones scattered on the surface. © by James Aronson

HOMINIDS

All human beings are hominids, but not all hominids are human beings.

According to the dictionary, a hominid is any of a family (Hominidae) of bipedal (upright walking) primate mammals consisting of recent man, his immediate ancestors, and related forms. The scientific community has had to leave some wiggle room in the precise definition of *hominid* because scientists still don't know exactly when the first hominid appeared. Chimpanzees and apes, though they share a distant ancestor with humans, are not hominids because they are not bipedal.

An elbow cast. The first fossil bone that caught Johanson's eye.
© by Donald Johanson, Institute of Human Origins

They had it, all right. They just had no idea what "it" was. One thing was certain: it was tiny—like a child—and completely unique. It appeared to be unlike any other hominid ever found. Its jaws were primitive, more like a chimpanzee's; yet its bowl-shaped pelvis was more modern, closer to a human's. It was small-brained, yet the pelvis suggested it had walked upright.

Early measurements and tests would reveal that the hominid was about three and a half feet tall. Its wisdom teeth had come in and showed several years of wear, which meant that it was not a child after all, but almost fully grown—probably in its twenties or late teens.

Discoverer Donald Johanson (left) and scientist Maurice Taieb
examine the newly discovered bones back at the field tent.
© by Donald Johanson, Institute of Human Origins

"We know in our species when those things [like teeth erupting] happen,"
explains Dirk Van Tuerenhout, curator at the Houston Museum of Natural
Science. "Then you start applying that knowledge to the fossils. But that
is assuming [they] grew along the same trajectory as modern humans—
[which] is not necessarily a given, but it's the best we can do."

THEORY OF EVOLUTION

In 1859, biologist Charles Darwin published his famous study *On the Origin of Species.*
In it, he proposed that humans in the past differed from modern humans. Darwin
hypothesized that all living species have evolved over great lengths of time (millions
of years). In other words, modern humans descended from some earlier, different
form of human.

In 1863, Thomas Henry Huxley published *Man's Place in Nature.* He proposed that
humans did not evolve from living (modern) apes, but rather humans and apes have
(and are descended from) a common ancestor. The hominid fossil record to date
continues to support this theory.

Finding answers, figuring out exactly who and what the hominid was, would take some time. Luckily, the hominid would help. Any scientist involved in paleontology would tell you that even though a creature has been dead for millions of years, "the bones still speak to you." Through its fossilized bones, scientists would say, "it" talks to them.

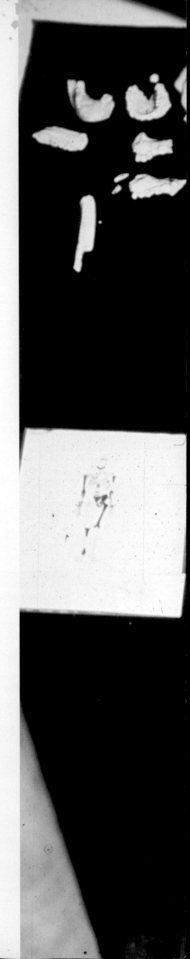

AND THE BONES SAID . . .

First, because the bones were scattered on the surface in one small place and there were no duplicate bones, it was clear that all the bones belonged to a single hominid. This was critical information, since most hominid fossils discovered previously were just bone fragments or a single fossil or two.

With more bones to study, scientists would be able to make a stronger case for their final analysis. Also crucial to that analysis would be the overall condition of the bones—which in this case was quite good. These bones were remarkably well preserved—protected both from the weathering process and from predators. Scientists are able to gather much more information from a bone that is in good shape.

"There were no tooth marks on [its] bones," wrote Johanson. *"They had not been crunched and splintered, as they would have been if [it] had been killed by a lion or a saber-toothed cat. . . .[It] had already begun to show the onset of arthritis or some other bone ailment, on the evidence of deformation of [its] vertebrae."*

Because of the quality of the bones, scientists were able to conclude—with reasonable certainty—that the little hominid was almost fully grown at the time of its death.

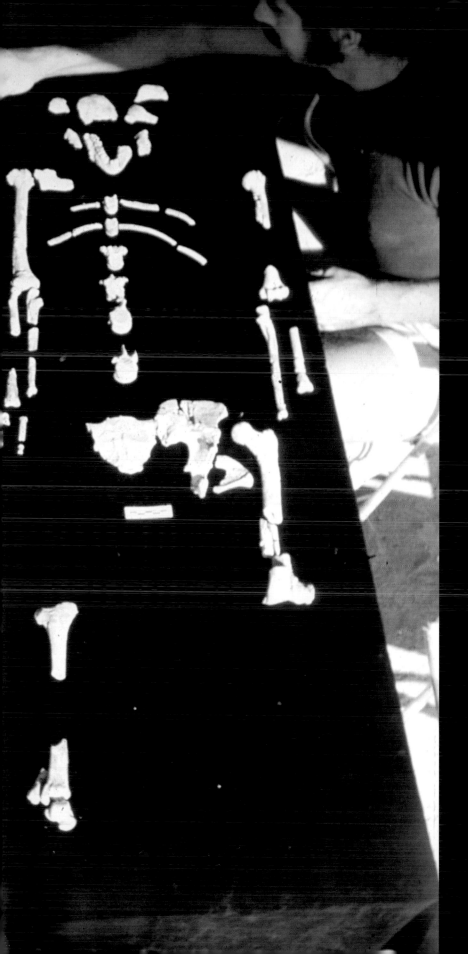

BOY OR GIRL?

"That afternoon everyone in camp was at the gully, sectioning off the site and preparing for a massive collecting job that ultimately took three weeks," explains Donald Johanson. *"When it was done, we had recovered several hundred pieces of bone (many of them fragments) representing about forty percent of the skeleton of a single individual."*

Donald Johanson lays out the bones in their correct anatomical positions.
© by James Aronson

Using rock hammers, dental tools, whisk-brooms, and screens to sift through piles of sediment, the team of scientists collected the skeleton bones. Erosion had already done the heavy work. Over time, the layers of rock had been worn away and the fossils had become dislodged. So the timing of the discovery was perfect, and the scientists needed only to pluck the exposed fossils from the surface. The team found a thighbone, ribs, vertebrae, and other fossil bones. Because the left and right sides of a skeleton are near replicas of each other, the scientists would be able to accurately reconstruct about seventy-five percent of the little hominid.

A worker in Hadar, Ethiopia, sifts through sediment, searching for any loose skeleton fragments.
© by David Brill

From the moment of discovery—based on initial observations—they were pretty sure, though not positive, that "it" was a girl. And though there was never any discussion or formal decision, after that frenzied first night of celebration and repeated playings of "Lucy in the Sky with Diamonds," "it" became known to the scientists, and to much of the world, as Lucy. In Ethiopia, her birthplace, she became known as Dinkenesh, meaning "beautiful one."

After preliminary measurements and observations were taken of the fossil bones while in Hadar, Johanson wrapped the priceless fossils in toilet paper, packed them carefully in a single carryon suitcase, and nestled it gently on his lap for the plane ride home. He brought the fossil bones to his lab in Cleveland, Ohio, where he and a team of colleagues took intricate measurements, wrote physical descriptions, and most important, constructed plaster casts of all the fossil remains.

FOSSILIZATION

Fossilization is an amazing and extremely rare occurrence. For the little hominid skeleton to have been preserved as a fossil, many elements had to come together at just the right time.

First, there had to be some water present to protect against rapid decomposition. (The hominid was found near a dried-up lake or riverbed.) The water (and loose sediments in it) protect the remains from bacteria and other forces that hasten the weathering and decaying process.

In addition, before predators and scavengers can find and eat the remains, the bones must be buried—for instance, from a lava flow or volcanic ash. The soft body tissues, like skin and muscles, eventually disintegrate and disappear (due to bacteria) and the hard bone is then left to be continually covered by layers of sediments (sand, mud, silt).

As the layers of sediment build up, the accumulated pressure turns the sediment into rock. Water, rich in minerals, trickles down through the sediments, whereupon the minerals dissolve away the hard bone and replace it with calcite or other minerals. This transformation process leaves hardened rock in the precise shape—often including fine details like muscle markings or bite indentations—of the original bone.

Wind, rain, floods, and even earthquakes eventually uncover some fossils. This movement of earth effectively unburies the fossilized bones and exposes them to view.

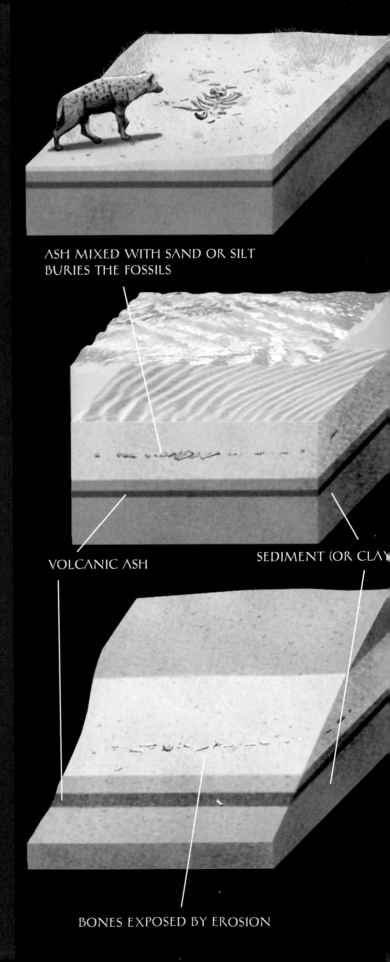

ASH MIXED WITH SAND OR SILT BURIES THE FOSSILS

VOLCANIC ASH

SEDIMENT (OR CLAY)

BONES EXPOSED BY EROSION

Fossil casts are precise replicas of the bones. Casts are made as back-ups, in case any damage comes to the original fossils. They also enable many scientists from different disciplines—anthropology, paleoanthropology, geology, geochronology—and even paleo-artists to study the bones and begin to unravel the mysteries that surround them.

AND THE BONES SAID . . .

One of the very first mysteries solved was that "it" was, as originally thought, unmistakenly female. But how can they tell girl bones from boy bones?

To the untrained eye, a bone looks like a bone, neither male nor female. But scientists know that in many species, females tend to have proportionately smaller bones than males. When Lucy was discovered, the glaring observation that her bones were so tiny was a strong indication that she was a girl.

"We determined that 'it' was a 'she' from the small stature, lightly built bones, and small canine [teeth] (inferred from the small root size) in her lower jaw," explains Johanson.

KNOWN SPECIES OR NEW?

Determining that Lucy was female was a key piece of the puzzle. But it was only the beginning. Who was this creature and what was she like? Was she more like a chimpanzee or closer to a human? Did she dwell in trees or walk upright?

"You go from the known and you work your way to the unknown," explains curator Dirk Van Tuerenhout at Houston's Museum of Natural Science. "So, for example, the best possible way to determine if a found fossil walked upright is to compare it to something we know walks upright—us. We do know how bipedality works, by studying ourselves."

At the time of her discovery, Lucy was the most complete, best-preserved skeleton of a hominid ever found. And because of this, she was arguably the most significant fossil discovery of the century.

SIGNIFICANT HOMINID DISCOVERIES

Prior to Lucy's discovery in 1974, only a handful of very old hominid specimens had been found. There was a piece of an arm bone, dated at 4 million years; a lower jaw fragment, at 5.5 million years; and a single hominid molar dated at 6 million years. Significant African hominid discoveries pre-Lucy included a skull nicknamed Taung Child (*Australopithecus africanus*) dated at 1–2 million years; a skull named Zinj (*Australopithecus boisei*) dated at 1.75 million years; and a cranium called 1470 (*Homo habilis*) that was dated at 1.9 million years.

 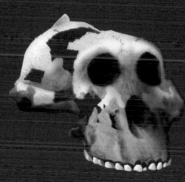 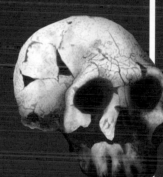

Taung Child   Zinj   1470

The most complete skeleton recovery of a hominid before Lucy was of a Neanderthal man who was a mere seventy-five thousand years old. All of the hominid reconstructions up to 1974 had been done using fragments of different individuals (of the same species) pieced together to make a complete whole. With Lucy, for the first time, almost the entire skeleton of a single hominid individual was there in one place.

Neanderthal man

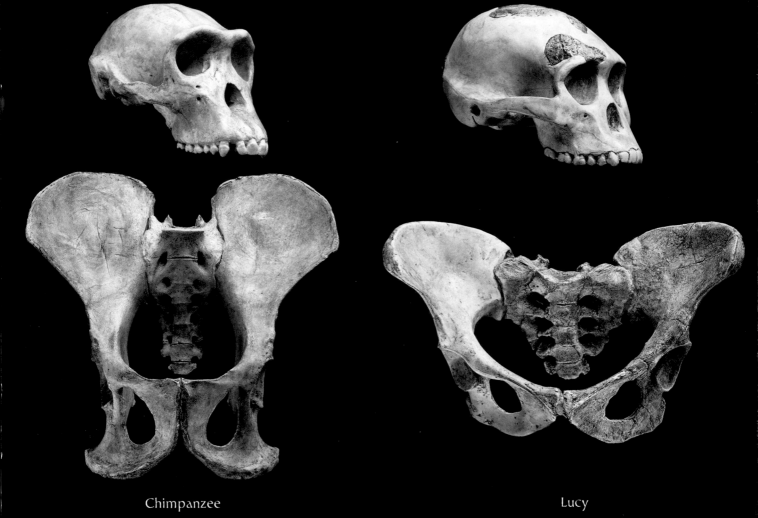

Chimpanzee

Lucy

And yet, she was still a pile of bones—making analysis a challenge. But by making comparative studies between species with similar characteristics (in the case of hominids, that means humans and chimpanzees and apes), it was possible to draw some conclusions and construct a theory about the unknown bones.

"We have the whole modern family tree," says curator Van Tuerenhout. "Gorillas, chimps, orangutans. We can look at them and see how they walk and wobble; how they can still climb trees; how they can do this and the other thing. You make a checklist; what kinds of traits can you identify?"

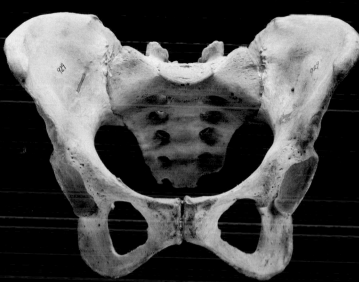

Modern human

The enormous importance of Lucy's discovery also rested on the differences between her various traits and those of any hominid ever previously found. She was small-brained, for example, yet it appeared she could walk upright. Before Lucy, it was thought that walking up-right evolved only *after* brain size increased. With Lucy, everything the scientists thought they knew about human evolution was suddenly thrown into question. They were staring at the established family tree, but were unable to see a branch to place the little hominid on.

Prior to Lucy, the human family tree was divided basically into two main hominid branches (after the split from apes had already occurred). On one branch was the Homo lineage (*H. habilis, H. erectus, H. sapiens*): hominids that were distinct ancestors of modern humans and displayed more modern traits, such as larger brains, smaller molars, and larger front teeth. On the other branch sat the South African australopithecines (*A. africanus, A. robustus*): hominids with more "primitive" features, including small brains, very big back teeth, and smaller front teeth.

2.5

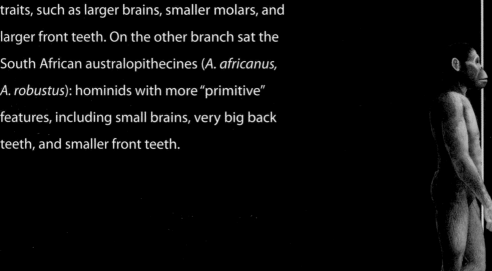

Australopithecus africanus

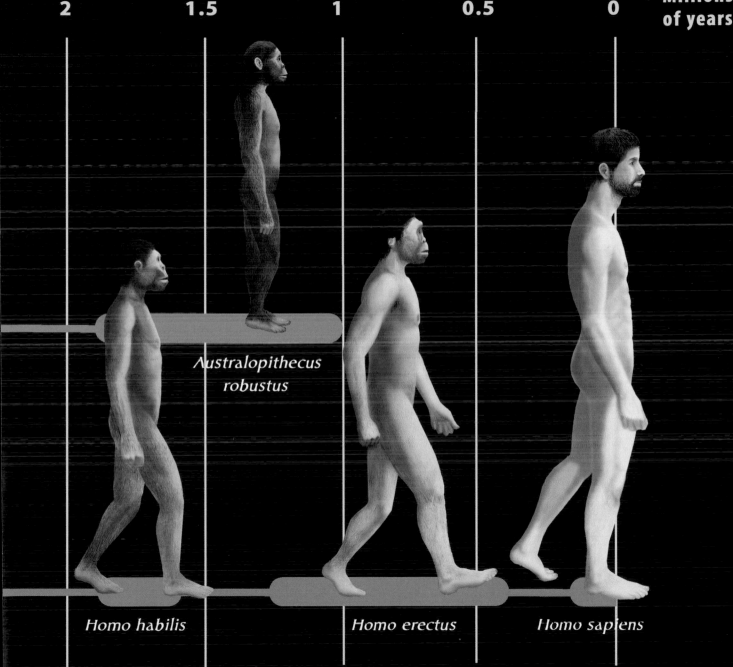

2   1.5   1   0.5   0   Millions of years

Australopithecus robustus

Homo habilis   *Homo erectus*   *Homo sapiens*

It was clear that Lucy wasn't on the Homo line: her bones were too tiny, her brain was too small, the proportions of her face were more apelike in appearance, and her palate shape and canine roots were also more apelike. The problem, though, was that she didn't fit the australopithecine mold either: Lucy had small molars and larger front teeth—distinctly human traits. Did she fit on the family tree? And if so, where?

In science, a theory is not a hunch; it is not guesswork. It is a detailed explanation that is based on a specific and precise approach to finding answers. Known as the scientific method, the approach works something like this: First, scientists make observations, such as these: Lucy's bones are very small; her brain is also quite small. Next are the hypothesis and the prediction: this hominid is therefore most likely an australopithecine. Then come the testing and modification of the hypothesis: this hominid has small molars and larger front teeth; those are traits associated with the Homo lineage. So the bones are saying that this hominid has traits found in both *Australopithecus* and *Homo*. Once the modified hypothesis is supported, in this case that Lucy is neither a known australopithecine nor homo, a conclusion—a theory—can be reached. The bones say Lucy is different from any other hominid previously discovered, and therefore a new species should be named.

AND THE BONES SAID . . .

After making detailed comparisons to chimpanzees, gorillas, and South African australopithecine specimens, the scientists concluded that Lucy was in fact a new kind of hominid. Because she appeared more apelike with human tendencies (as opposed to more human with apelike tendencies), Lucy was placed in the genus *Australopithecus.* But since she was different from the known australopithecines, she was given a new species name, *afarensis* (named for the region where she and, later, others of her species were found: the Afar Triangle in Ethiopia). In all, scientists eventually found fossils from more than three hundred individual *Australopithecus afarensis.* This abundance of fossils made them even more comfortable in their decision to name a new species.

ANCIENT OR MODERN?

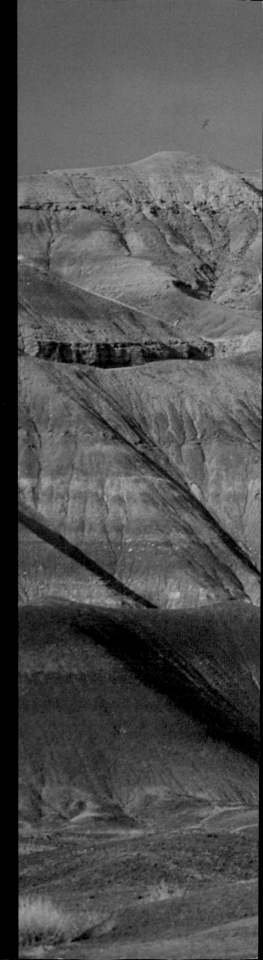

"We cannot date the fossils directly," notes geochronologist James Aronson, "because the fossilization process changes the bones themselves. The original bone has a history of being altered: going from a bone that is fairly light and porous on the interior to a fossil that is densely recrystalized by groundwater."

Without dating the fossils directly, how could scientists ever hope to uncover the ultimate mystery: the age of these bones? How could they know when this creature lived?

Hope lay in the rocks where the fossils came from. To determine Lucy's age, rock specialists (like geologists and geochronologists) turned their attention to the Hadar site where Lucy was found. Identifying the various layers of rock was step one. The rocks they were most interested in were on top of and just beneath the fossils, and had been built up over the course of millions of years. This process of identification is known as determining the stratigraphic column, or stratigraphic sequence—and it is critical in dating fossils.

A view of the stratigraphy—layering
of rock—at the site in Hadar.
© by Donald Johanson, Institute of Human Origins

Geochronologist James Aronson and his student Bob Walter study the stratigraphy of Hadar. They search for pristine rock samples to use for potassium-argon dating. © by David Brill

"With Lucy, working out the stratigraphy [the layers of rock] was pretty straightforward. It took a lot of effort, but it's a lot of fun to be out in the field," says Aronson.

Volcanic material—either a lava flow or volcanic ash—is the most reliable type of rock to date. That's because it forms at the very moment it is deposited, uncontaminated by other rocks and debris carried in by wind and water. At the Lucy site in Hadar, there was a layer of basalt (hardened lava) some distance below the area of the fossils and a volcanic ash layer much closer (about three meters below).

Attached to all the fossil bones was a coarse, white mixture of sand pebbles and granules that corresponded identically to a layer of sand slightly above the volcanic ash. This specific match was clear evidence that Lucy's bones had come from a layer of sand just above the ash, and at some recent point had been washed loose by floods and erosion. Scientists were now extremely confident they had placed Lucy's bones correctly in the stratigraphic column.

Step two, then, was gathering the rock samples for dating. Which is easier said than done.

"The major thing with Lucy," says Aronson, *"was to get below the zone of weathering and find fresh, unweathered rock, which is very hard [to do]."*

But they were able to collect several samples of unweathered basalt and samples of the volcanic ash—which, because of its closeness to the fossils, was critical. Next was the dating process. The scientists used a complex system called potassium-argon dating, which measures amounts of the elements potassium and argon in the volcanic rock sample.

A rock sample from the Hadar site is heated, and melted, in the potassium-argon dating system. The melting releases all the argon trapped in the rock. The amount of argon determines the age of the rock. © by James Aronson

"The age is a direct function of the amount of argon and potassium," explains Aronson. *"Inside the [potassium-argon dating] system, we can heat up the rock sample and melt it so that it gives off any argon that has been produced in the history of that rock."*

The more argon a sample has, the older it is. Certain minerals work better than others for dating purposes. Feldspar crystals (found in the volcanic material) are the most reliable, because they are not as subjected to the weathering process (which causes alterations).

The scientists tried to measure as many different varieties of feldspar crystals as they could, looking for consistent readings of argon. One type of sample for Lucy was particularly good: the volcanic ash with abundant feldspar that appeared on top of every fossil unit. (Erosion caused the fossils to mix with the ash below it.) Because the many samples yielded consistent dates, the scientists were fairly comfortable with the age they ultimately assigned to Lucy . . . and indeed, she was ancient.

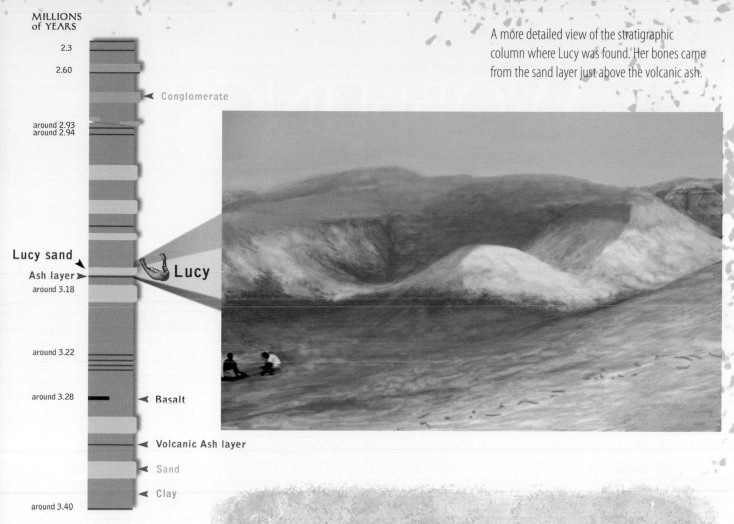

MILLIONS
of YEARS

2.3
2.60

◄ Conglomerate

around 2.93
around 2.94

Lucy sand ►

Ash layer ►

around 3.18

Lucy

around 3.22

around 3.28 ◄ Basalt

◄ Volcanic Ash layer

◄ Sand

◄ Clay

around 3.40

A more detailed view of the stratigraphic column where Lucy was found. Her bones came from the sand layer just above the volcanic ash.

AND THE BONES SAID . . .

So how old is old?

Lucy's bones were able to answer this question based on their burial spot within the stratigraphic sequence.

Their age came in initially at 3.5 million years. But further tests proved this number to be too high. Several years after the discovery, a refined potassium-argon technique was applied, dating Lucy to 3.2 million years ago—making Lucy the oldest, most complete fossil skeleton ever found.

"The sand unit that contained Lucy is only a few meters above the precisely dated . . . volcanic ash [3.18 million years]," Aronson further explains. "We judge the sand is only about ten thousand years younger [than the ash]."

WOBBLING OR WALKING?

Was Lucy bipedal? Did she walk easily on two legs or simply wobble about and live mostly in trees? Many scientists believe that the development of upright walking was a key element in human evolution because it freed the hands for other uses—like tool-making, which in turn powered brain growth. So the question—and the answer—were critical to the evolutionary mystery.

"It's not just looking at a bone and measuring how long it is," explains *biological anthropologist Owen Lovejoy. "It's looking very intensively at its structure—all the little nooks and crannies and things that stick out and stick in. Because they tell you what was attached there, how big it was, and how it operated on the bone."*

Now it was up to experts like Owen Lovejoy (who specializes in skeletal mechanics, or how the skeleton moves) to find out. Before Lucy was discovered, upright walking was thought to have developed *after* brain size increased: a larger-brained animal was thought to be capable of more complex actions, like walking. But here was Lucy: 3.2 million years old, still small-brained, and possibly bipedal.

Owen Lovejoy, an expert on locomotion
studies x-rays of leg bones showing the
mechanics of walking. © by David Bril

Even though so many of Lucy's fossilized bones were found, they
weren't all in one piece due to the amount of time and weathering
that had passed. So Lovejoy's first order of business was to reconstruct
the pelvis—which was found in approximately forty fragments fused
together in a fossilized ball and was also missing the left pelvic bone.

Once he pulled apart the jumbled fragments and reconstructed the right side, he would make a mirror-image cast of the left pelvic bone to create the full pelvis. It wasn't possible for him to pick away at the matrix directly (the solidified mix of sand and silt that had initially buried the bones), because that would have destroyed the fossil. So he outlined each individual fragment in the mass, and made an individual cast of every fragment.

"What you do is make a cast of the fossilized mass," explains Lovejoy. *"Then you take a separate cast and each time work out what a different piece looked like. You start anew every time, reconstructing each of the pieces separately. And then you end up with all the pieces of the original and you glue those back together to see what they look like."*

CASTS

The plaster casts made of Lucy's fossilized bones are so good, so precise and accurate in detail, that you could perform electron microscopy on them (using a high-powered microscope to show details unseen to the naked eye). The cast-making process doesn't hurt the original fossil bone at all. Several steps are involved in making a cast:

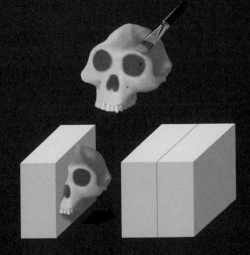

1. Paint several layers (up to thirty) of a liquid rubber polymer on the fossil bone.
2. Take that whole thing and cover it with plaster, creating the mother mold.

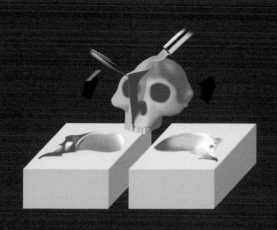

3. Break the mother mold away and cut away the rubber.

4. Place the rubber mold into the plaster mold to keep it rigid; the rubber will have preserved all the intricate details of the fossil.

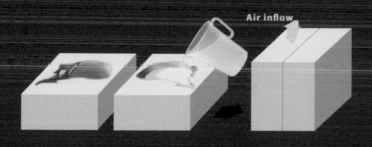

Air inflow

5. Pour plaster inside the two rubber halves and press them together, continually moving air through (with a machine) so that as the material is drying it is distributed evenly to all three dimensions of the bone.

6. When it is dry, open the two halves of the mold and you are left with a perfect cast of the fossilized bone.

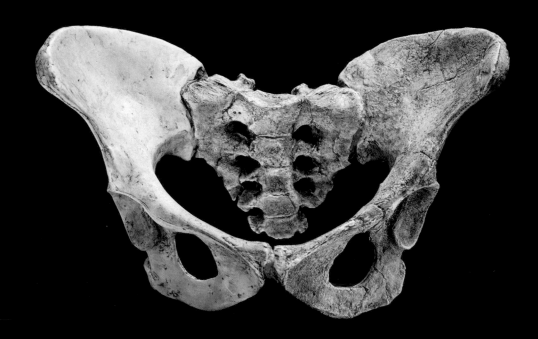

But how would scientists know if they got the pieces back together correctly? How could they tell if it was an accurate reconstruction of the pelvis? In Lucy's case, they were confident for three reasons:

1) The pieces were preserved at their natural break points, making them fit together easily without forcing.

2) The internal and external surfaces of the pelvis had distinct impressions, and when glued together they fused to make an anatomically correct pelvis.

3) When the left and right sides of the pelvis were put against the sacrum (the fused vertebrae between the pelvic hip bones), the front parts met at the midline, which is the accurate placement.

Using comparative anatomy (looking at other hominids, modern humans and chimpanzees and gorillas) and tools like x-rays and CT scans, the scientists focused on Lucy's pelvis and leg bone (femur). Later, they studied other bones (like the heel bone) of other members of her species. In the past three hundred years, orthopedic specialists and anatomists have done innumerable studies that describe all the adaptations in the human skeleton that make upright walking easy for us.

Eventually, the scientists showed that all of those same adaptations in the human skeleton were present in Lucy. For example, her ilia (pelvic bones) were relatively short, compared to the ilia of a chimpanzee. This shortening lowered the body's center of mass, which made it easier to keep upright. The ilia were also curved, which helped to stabilize the pelvis when Lucy stood on one leg.

"Not only did she have the parts," explains Lovejoy, "not only do they look like the same parts in humans, but we know that they were working in the same fashion, based on markings of how the muscles and tendons were attached [to the bone]."

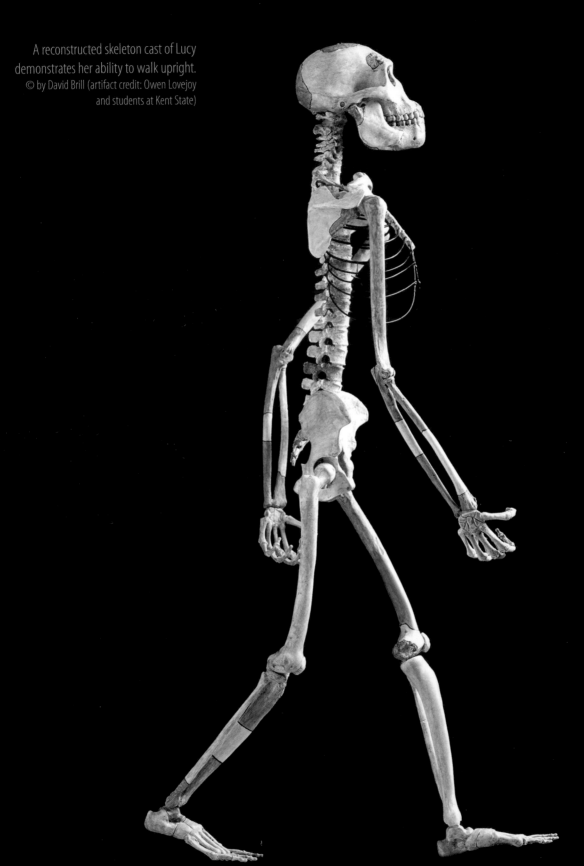

A reconstructed skeleton cast of Lucy demonstrates her ability to walk upright. © by David Brill (artifact credit: Owen Lovejoy and students at Kent State)

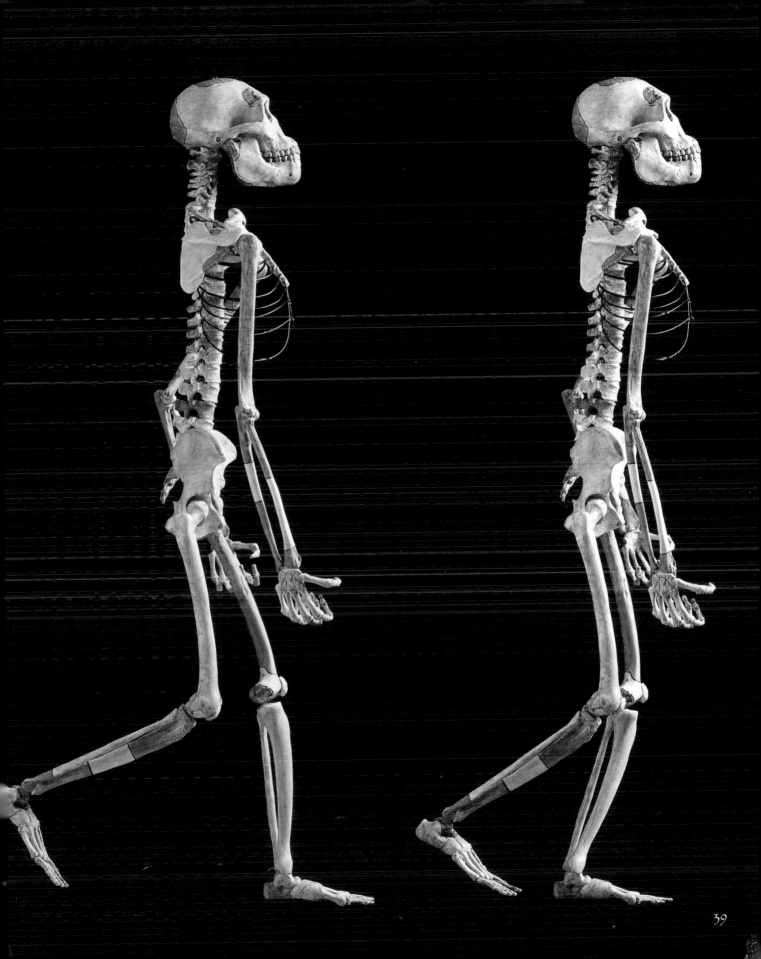

One question that remains is, why? Why did Lucy and her small-brained species decide one day that they would move about on two legs, thus freeing their arms for other uses? Why did they decide to leave the trees and become upright walking bipeds?

One of the oldest hypotheses still floating around is that as the hominids left the forests and moved onto open savannah, they needed to stand up to see over tall grasses to scan for predators. This concept, though, is not widely accepted today. Another idea is that hominids needed to free their hands for making and using tools. Lucy's discovery did not directly support this theory: she could walk, but there is no evidence she used tools—there were no tool artifacts found near her or any of her species.

There are other possibilities, but one hypothesis put forth by Owen Lovejoy—and deemed plausible by many in the scientific community—revolves around the notion of food sharing as part of a larger survival strategy. In this scenario, the male goes in search of food not only for himself but also for his mate, who stays behind, conserving her energy. With more time and energy, the female is able to care for her offspring—bettering their chances of survival. According to this hypothesis, the males stood upright to free their arms for carrying food, and then put one foot in front of the other in order to bring it back.

But since fossils don't show behavioral patterns, no one knows for sure why hominids became bipedal. One thing though is certain. The only mammals in the history of the world to stand upright and walk on two legs are Lucy, other hominids, and modern humans.

AND THE BONES SAID . . . .

So Lucy could walk well?

Her pelvic bone rises above the hip joint and allows her hip muscles to steady her body during each step. Her upper leg bones angle outward, positioning her knees for support. Her species has a heel bone that's inflated just like a modern human's—an energy-absorption mechanism that other primates don't have.

"There's no question whatsoever that she was a complete and well-adapted biped," asserts Owen Lovejoy. "That's what her big shock was. You take that pelvis, and you compare it to that [small] brain and you say, 'What the heck is going on here?' She is not at all what the world expected."

To create the image, Gurche first had to reconstruct Lucy's entire skeleton to use as the base for his sculpture. Using casts of the original fossil bones, and the knowledge that a skeleton is a near mirror-image of itself (right side and left side), he was able to restore the body to a close approximation of its original structure. In building a life-size hominid, Gurche brought to his process twenty years of experience: experience dissecting human cadavers and great apes. That told him a great deal about how to interpret a skeleton in terms of how soft tissues—like muscles and tendons—attached to it.

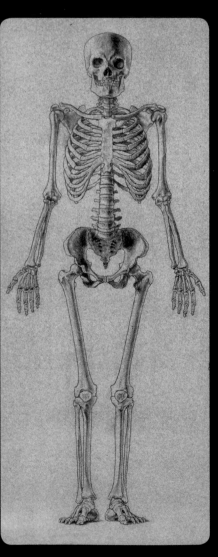

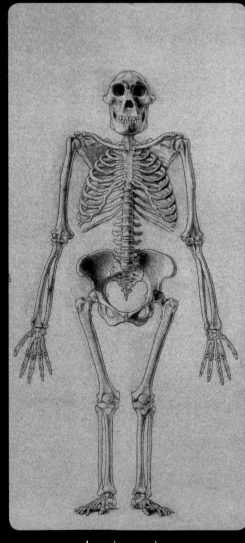

Homo sapien

Lucy's species

"You can look at muscle markings [on the bones] and get an idea of how powerful the various muscles were," explains Gurche. "All other things being equal, a more powerful muscle will stimulate, will cause, bone growth at the site of attachment. A really strongly marked bone is a hint that it might be a really well developed muscle. You try to let the science take you as far as it can."

From left to right, artist John Gurche compares the male skeletons of *Homo sapiens* (modern humans); Lucy's species, *Australopithecus afarensis*; the hominid *Australopithecus africanus*; and a chimpanzee.
© by John Gurche

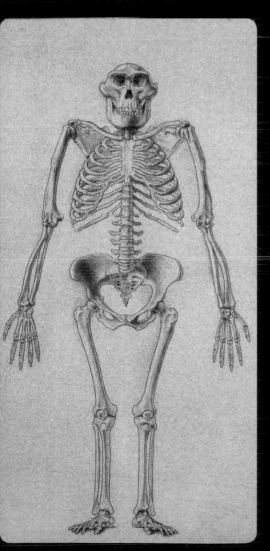

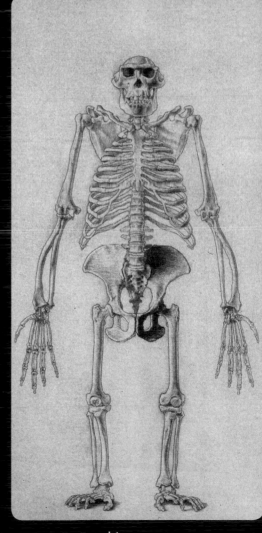

A. Africanus   chimpanzee

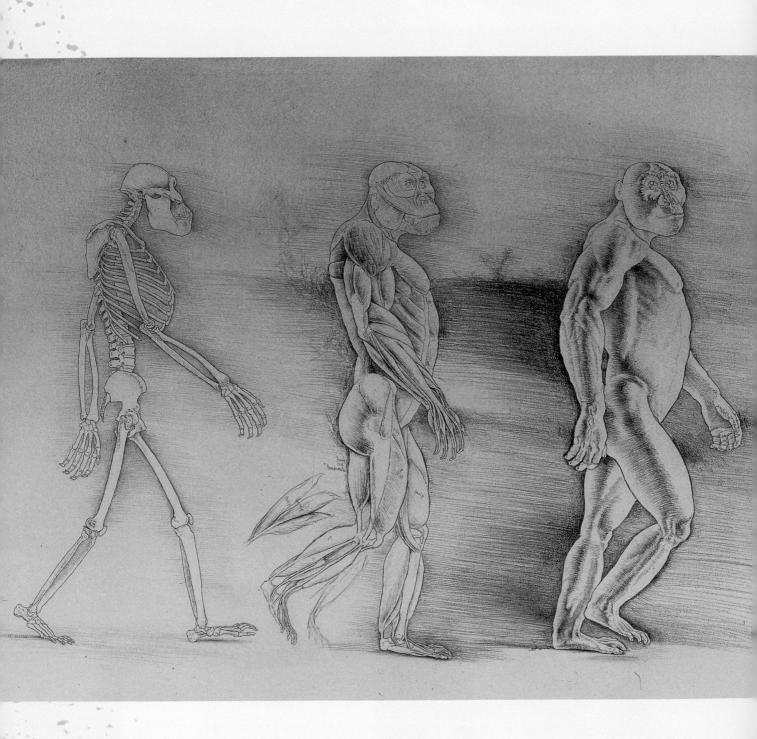

Lucy's skeleton was so complete that the artists were able to get a really good idea of the dimensions of her trunk and the correct proportions of her arms and legs. They could see she was small but powerful.

"There's some interpretation involved in getting the subtleties of the muscle shape down," says Gurche. "You keep a left eyeball on human anatomy and African ape anatomy, just for certain points of reference. Then, using a little bit of artistic license, you can sculpt in clay over the cast of the skeleton."

Gurche built Lucy up muscle by muscle, using a type of clay that doesn't dry. Once her shape was complete, he made molds of it—first a silicone mold, then a second, supporting mold of heavy-duty dental plaster. Next, he poured a durable but lifelike urethane plastic material into the mold to create the final form. And then he began the process of bringing it to life. Of course no modern human had seen this species before, so how could it possibly be reconstructed? Actually, most of the decisions were educated guesses based on prior knowledge; again, working from the known to the unknown.

Artist John Gurche sketches *Australopithecus afarensis* (Lucy's species) as a progression. First come the skeleton bones, the size, shape, and indentations of which inform how much muscle mass the individual probably had, which in turn dictates the final form of the life-size sculpture (or drawing).
© by John Gurche

Take, for instance, Lucy's skin color. Skin color in modern humans is not a big mystery. Though other factors may be at play, it appears that there is a direct correlation between skin color and the amount of sunlight a body is exposed to in any given latitude (how close to the equator, north or south, a person is). Skin color in people near the equator tends to be darker, and Lucy lived pretty close to the equator. Her hair—the color, texture, and how much coverage—required more guesswork, but even that was informed by science.

"I gave Lucy a coat of hair that is sort of in between what you'd get in a sparsely haired chimp and a very hairy human," explains Gurche. "We just don't know for sure, but that was my best guess."

He based his guess on the assumptions that Lucy and her species were spending some of their time in open environments and some in more closed environments. An open savannah is indicated by the fossil remains of plants and animals of that period, whereas Lucy's long arms, curved fingers, and upward-tilted shoulders suggest to some that she still spent time in trees.

Gurche used black bear hair because it closely resembles chimpanzee hair. To get the hair on the figure, and to make it look convincing, he had to punch in each hair, one by one, with a needle.

The entire sculpture took about fifteen months to complete. Reconstructing Lucy's face was critical, and the task was complicated because most of her skull was not preserved. Luckily, several good specimens of *afarensis* were found at Hadar, not far from where Lucy was discovered.

"My first step," Gurche says, *"was to build a composite skull from some of the smaller cranial remains that were known."*

Hand-making Lucy's eyes alone was about a thirty-five-step process. Pressure and heat were used to mold the acrylic for the eyeballs, and various elements, such as the iris, were painted on separate pieces of acrylic. Capturing all the complexities, and then fusing them together, was one of Gurche's greatest challenges.

"Getting the eyes right is important," Gurche says. *"That's where the impression of a living, sentient creature is going to come from."*

The time commitment, though, was well worth it. As Gurche and the other scientists explain, they knew that in the end, it would be the image of this hominid—and the realization that she may be our ancestor—that would spark the imagination of the people who learned of her. It is the image that really transports us back in time and brings to mind a very different world.

It is the image that really makes us wonder . . . is *that* what Lucy looked like?

Paleo-artist John Gurche's
life-size sculpture of what Lucy probably
looked like. © by John Gurche

LUCY

Long ago, Lucy lived. Her skeleton remains have told us many things.
We know, for instance, that her arms were proportionately longer than
her legs, suggesting that, even though she was fully bipedal, she still
spent time in trees—perhaps to sleep or hide from predators. It is clear
from the wear on her teeth that she was a savannah omnivore, feasting
on berries and nuts and vegetation as she roamed about day by day.

Though her bones speak, they can't tell us everything. Big questions remain unanswered. Could Lucy talk? What types of sounds might she have made? Though no direct evidence was found, we still wonder if she made or used tools, such as a hammer for cracking open nuts, or a stone weapon for protection. The idea that she and her species shared food with one another, and thus perhaps were pair-bonded (had a single mate), suggests they might have had a community of sorts. Some of the evidence points in this direction, but it hasn't been proved.

And of course, that most intriguing set of questions still lingers: What kinds of feelings or emotions, if any, did Lucy have? Did she love her child or her mate? Did she cry tears of sadness? Did she experience joy or laughter? All we can do is wonder.

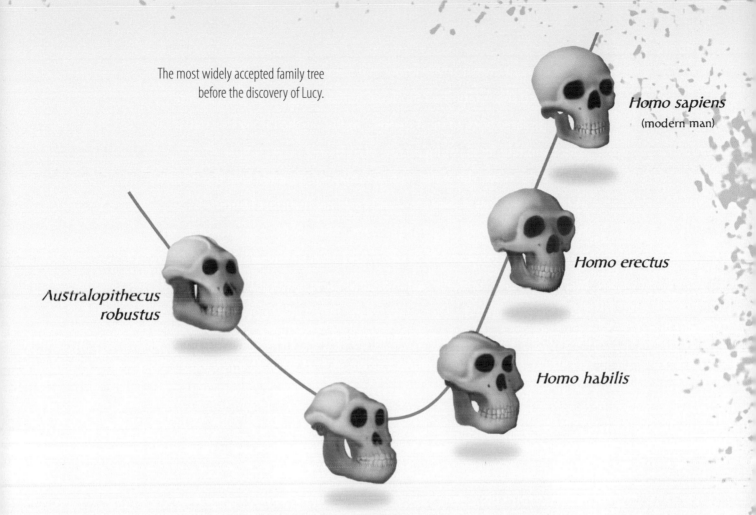

The most widely accepted family tree before the discovery of Lucy.

Homo sapiens
(modern man)

Homo erectus

Australopithecus robustus

Homo habilis

Australopithecus africanus

In the early days of paleoanthropology, the prevailing wisdom was that we were searching for a missing link. It was thought that there was one species somewhere in the distant past that marked the exact point when humans split from apes. (About eight to ten million years ago, apes and humans took different evolutionary paths. A lack of fossil evidence so far makes it impossible to pinpoint this split.) Evolution was thought to be a fairly linear tract, a straight line, with one species evolving into another species, which evolved into this and then that. By the time of Lucy's discovery, however, scientists knew they were searching for ancestors and cousins of modern humans, not a single "missing link."

So is Lucy our ancestor? We know that Lucy's discovery dramatically rearranged the established model of human origins, and that it came as a complete shock to most people. Suddenly, the family tree had a very complete fossil sitting on one of its branches. A complete fossil that would "wow" the world with her uniqueness, and claim the throne as one of the most significant—and certainly the most famous— hominid fossil ever found. The previous ideas of who our ancestors were, and what traits evolved when, and what defines a human in the first place, were suddenly cast in an intriguing new light. By naming Lucy a new hominid—she clearly wasn't *Homo* or a known australo- pithicine—and then placing her on the already crowded family tree, scientists demonstrated, in one fell swoop, that several competing ideas about the antiquity (the age) of modern humans no longer held up.

This new family tree showed that humans were descended from a hominid form not nearly as old as many would have liked to believe. (Some paleoanthropologists—enamored with the idea that humans populated the earth far back in time—wanted to believe the human line stretched back seven, eight, even ten million years.) This family tree slapped down the widely held belief that brain growth was the beginning developmental trait in human evolution. Rather, the first major step in becoming human was actually taking the first step— walking upright.

One generally accepted contemporary version of the human family tree. As new discoveries are made, the tree must be rearranged or even changed. The family tree, which is more like a bush, constantly changes as new evidence is uncovered.

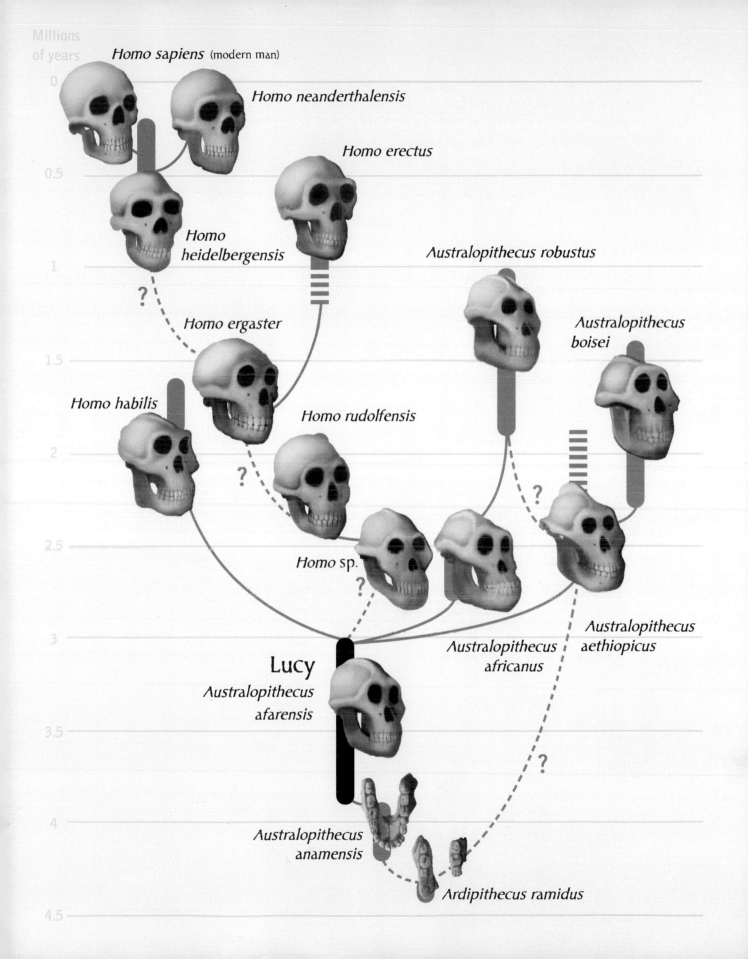

Millions of years

0

0.5

1

1.5

2

2.5

3

3.5

4

4.5

Homo sapiens (modern man)

Homo neanderthalensis

Homo erectus

Homo heidelbergensis

Australopithecus robustus

Australopithecus boisei

?

Homo ergaster

Homo habilis

Homo rudolfensis

?

?

Homo sp.

?

Australopithecus aethiopicus

Lucy
Australopithecus afarensis

Australopithecus africanus

?

Australopithecus anamensis

Ardipithecus ramidus

And because Lucy's species is the only hominid (known thus far) to have existed between three and four million years ago, this new family tree placed *Australopithecus afarensis* as the presumed ancestor to *Homo*. As it turns out, though, it has become increasingly clear that there really is no such thing as a human family *tree*. The variety of hominid fossil records, coupled with studies of other branches of evolutionary science (like mitochondrial DNA analysis and paleoneurology), bring into focus a family tree that is really more like a *bush*.

Different branches of species evolved and became extinct; there is no single, linear tract. Human evolution, it appears, came about in fits and starts. And as new fossil or DNA evidence is unearthed, interpretations and hominid placements on the family bush may be rearranged or even changed. (If, for example, a hominid is discovered that coexisted with *afarensis*, Lucy may then turn out to be more of a cousin—related to *Homo*, but not ancestral.)

Today, the mystery continues: *Where did we come from?* Luckily, we now have a three-and-a-half-foot-tall, long-armed, short-legged clue. A clue that sported primitive jaws—like a chimpanezee's—but boasted a modern pelvis—very much like a human's. A clue that shocked with the unimaginable: a small (chimp like) brain along with the (human-like) abililty to walk upright.

Where did we come from? The answer is still unknown . . . but now we have a magnificent clue.

Because somewhere deep in the past, near the beginning, lived Lucy.

A life-size sculpture of Lucy created
by paleo-artist John Gurche. © by John Gurche

GLOSSARY

anthropology: the study of humanity.

anatomy: a branch of biology concerned with the structure of living things.

anatomical: refers to the structures of a body.

ancestor: one from whom a person is descended.

argon: a chemical element with the periodic table symbol Ar. It is a noble (inactive or inert) gas and is colorless. Argon is present in the atmosphere, but at less than 1 percent.

australopithecine: any of a genus of extinct southern African hominids with a relatively small brain; *Australopithecus* is the genus name, while *australopithecine* refers to an individual creature.

bipedal: walking upright on two legs.

cadaver: a dead body.

decompose: to undergo a chemical breakdown; to decay or rot.

DNA analysis: DNA (deoxyribonucleic acid) contains the genetic imprint used in the development and functioning of all known living organisms. DNA analysis studies and tests human and animal DNA samples.

evolution: the theory that all living plants and animals originated from other, preexisting types of plants and animals.

evolutionary science: a combination of modern biology and evolution history.

evolve: to undergo evolutionary change.

gene: an element in the DNA that controls the transmission of hereditary traits, or traits that get passed down from one generation to another.

genus: a category of biological classification ranking below a family and above a species. For example, Lucy is part of the human family tree and part of the genus *Australopithecus*, but is a new species—*afarensis*.

geology: the study of solid matter that makes up rocks, soil, and gemstones.

geochronology: the science of determining the age of rocks, fossils, and sediments.

hominid: see page 9

homo: any of a genus of primate mammals that includes modern man and several extinct, related species.

lineage: a group of individuals who trace direct descent from a common ancestor.

mitochondrial DNA: the DNA found in a cell's mitochondria (long, cellular organelles found outside a cell's nucleus).

paleo-: ancient.

paleoanthropology: the study of ancient humans and human origins.

paleo-artist: an artist who specializes in creating art that is representative of prehistoric time periods.

paleoneurology: the study of brain impressions on prehistoric skulls.

paleontology: the study of prehistoric life forms.

primate: any of an order of mammals comprising man together with apes, monkeys, and related forms.

potassium: a chemical element with the periodic table symbol K. It is an alkali metal and is silvery white in appearance.

species: a group that has common attributes and is designated by a common name.

stratigraphy: rock layers and layering.

trajectory: the path an object follows.

ACKNOWLEDGMENTS

The author would like to acknowledge and thank the following people:

Donald Johanson for his discovery of Lucy, his contribution of photos and quotations, and his time in reviewing the manuscript for accuracy.

Interview subjects **James Aronson, John Gurche, C. Owen Lovejoy,** and **Dirk Van Tuerenhout** for sharing their time and expertise and reviewing the manuscript for accuracy.

David Brill, John Gurche, James Aronson, and **Donald Johanson** for supplying the magnificent photos.

Oscar Sanisidro for the fabulous illustrations.

Lydia Zelaya of Simon and Schuster and **Jose Barrera Flores** of the Institute for Human Origins for their assistance with permissions and gathering materials.

My husband, Paul, and kids, **Jaimie** and **Simon,** for their ongoing support.

The team at Houghton Mifflin, who helped make this book the best it could be.

My magnificent editor, **Ann Rider,** who, after working on five books with me, still consistently provides keen insight and astute commentary . . . and is simply a joy to work with.

SOURCES

QUOTED SOURCES
Tape-recorded interviews: James Aronson, John Gurche, Owen Lovejoy, Dirk Van Tuerenhout.

Johanson, Donald C., and Maitland A. Edey. *Lucy: The Beginnings of Humankind*. New York: Simon and Schuster, 1981. Excerpted by permission of Simon and Schuster Adult Publishing Group.

SOURCES
Books:
Fagan, Brian M., ed. *Eyewitness to Discovery*. New York: Oxford University Press, 1996.

Johanson, Donald, and Blake Edgar. *From Lucy to Language*. A Peter N. Nevraumont Book. New York: Simon and Schuster, 1996.

Johanson, Donald, Lenora Johanson, and Blake Edgar. *Ancestors: In Search of Human Origins*. New York: Villard Books, 1994.

Johanson, Donald, and James Shreeve. *Lucy's Child: The Discovery of a Human Ancestor*. New York: Avon Books, 1989.

Sloan, Christopher. *The Human Story: Our Evolution from Prehistoric Ancestors to Today*. Washington, D.C.: National Geographic Society, 2004.

Tattersall, Ian. *The Fossil Trail*. New York: Oxford University Press, 1995.

Articles:
Begley, Sharon. "Beyond Stones and Bones." *Newsweek* (March 19, 2007): 53–59.

Johanson, D. C. "Ethiopia Yields First Family of Early Man." *National Geographic* 150, no. 6 (December 1976): 790–811.

———. "Face to Face with Lucy's Family." *National Geographic* 189, no. 3 (March 1996): 96–117.

Johanson, D. C., and T. D. White. "A Systematic Assessment of Early African Hominids." *Science* 203 (January 26, 1979): 321–330.

Lovejoy, C. Owen. "Evolution of Human Walking." *Scientific American* (November 1988): 118–25.

Waters, Tom. "Almost Human." *Discover* (May 1990): 44–53.

DVD-ROM
Biography: Charles Darwin; Evolution's Voice. DVD-ROM. A&E Television Networks, 1998.

From Ape to Man. DVD-ROM. The History Channel, A&E Television Networks, 2005.

In Search of Human Origins. Parts 1–3. DVD-ROM. NOVA Special, PBS, 1997.

WEBSITES
The Institute for Human Origins. www.asu.edu/clas/iho.
Becoming Human. www.becominghuman.org.
The Human Origins Program at the Smithsonian Institute. www.mnh.si.edu/anthro/humanorigins.
Hall of Human Origins; American Museum of Natural History. www.amnh.org/education/resources/exhibitions/humanorigins/educators.php?src=h_nc.
Department of Human Evolution, Max Planck Institute for Evolutionary Anthropology. www.eva.mpg.de/evolution/index.htm.

INDEX

Afar Triangle, 25
apes, 11, 20, 25, 37
Ardipithecus ramidus, 57
argon, 29–30, *30*
Aronson, James, 26, *28,* 29, 30
Australopithecus, 55
Australopithecus aethiopicus, 57
Australopithecus afarensis, 25, *44, 47, 49, 57*
Australopithecus africanus, 19, *19,* 22, *22, 45, 57*
Australopithecus anamensis, 57
Australopithecus boisei, 19, *19, 57*
Australopithecus robustus, 22, *23, 55, 57*

bipedal motion. *See* walking

calcite, 10
casts, plaster, *10,* 15, 17, 34–35, *34–35,* 44
chimpanzee, 20, *20,* 25, 37, *45*
CT scan, 37

Darwin, Charles, 11
Dinkenesh, 15
DNA tests, 58

Ethiopia, *3,* 25. *See also* Hadar
evolution, human: importance of Lucy, 21, 56; theory after Lucy, 56, *56,* 58; theory before Lucy, 22, *22, 55,* 55–56
evolutionary science, 58

family tree. *See* evolution, human
feldspar, 30
food, carrying, 41
fossilization, *4, 5,* 16, *16,* 26
fossil record, 11, 55
fossils: artistic interpretation, 43, 50, *50;* dating, 26–31; formation (*see* fossilization); male vs. female, 17; threats to preservation, 12, 14, 16
1470, 19, *19*

geology and fossil dating. *See* stratigraphic column
glossary, 60–61
gorilla, 20, 25, 37
Gray, Tom, 8
Gurche, John: creation of image, 43–51; reconstructed sculpture of Lucy by, *50, 58*

Hadar, Ethiopia: geology and fossil dating, 26–31, *27, 28, 30, 31;* Lucy fossil site, *8,* 13, *14;* map, *3*
hominid: definition, 9; discoveries, 19, *19;* evolution, 22, *22;* Lucy as a new species, 18, 20–21, 24–25, 56
Hominidae, 9
Homo erectus, 22, *23, 55, 57*
Homo ergaster, 57
Homo habilis, 19, *19,* 22, *23, 55, 57*
Homo heidelbergensis, 57
Homo neanderthalensis, 57
Homo rudolfensis, 57
Homo sapiens, 22, *23, 44, 55, 57*
Homo sp., 57
human, modern: comparison of fossils with, 11, 18, 37; evolution (*See* evolution, human); pelvis and skull, *21;* shared ancestor with apes, 11; *vs.* hominids, 9; *See also Homo sapiens*
Huxley, Thomas Henry, 11

Johanson, Donald, 7–8, *11,* 15

Lovejoy, Owen: cast-making, 34, *36;* skeleton research, 32, *33, 36,* 37, 42; theory on walking, 41
Lucy: age at death, 10, 12; arthritis, 12; brain, 10, 21, 24, 32; creation of image, 43–51, *45;* diet, 53; eyes, 49–50; face, 49–50, *50;* as female, 15, 17; habitat, 48, *52,* 53; hair, 48, 49; height, 10; importance to paleontology, 18, 21, 56; local name, 15; as a new hominid species, 18, 20–21, 24–25; origin of name, 7, 15; reconstructed sculpture of, *50, 58;* skin color, 48; social aspects, 54; unanswered questions about, 54; walking, 10, 21, 32–42, *38;* see also *Australopithecus afarensis*
Lucy fossil bones: age, 31; analysis, 10, *11,* 12, 15; arms, 48, 53; dating, 26–31; discovery, 7–8, *8;* elbow, *10;* fingers, 48; heel, 37, 42; jaw, 10; leg, 37, 42; move to U.S. lab, 15; palate, 24; pelvis, 10, *20, 33, 36,* 36–37, 42; percent that was found, 13; percent that was reconstructed, 14; ribs, 14; shoulders, 48; skeleton, *6, 13, 44,* 44–45, *47;* skull, *20,* 49; teeth, 10,

17, 24, 53; thigh, 14; uniqueness, 10–12, 56, 58; vertebrae, 12, 14
"Lucy in the Sky with Diamonds" (song), 7, 15

Man's Place in Nature (book), 11
"missing link," 55
muscles and tendons, 16, 32, 42, 44–45, 47, *47*
Neanderthal man, 19, *19.* See also *Homo neanderthalensis*

On the Origin of Species (book), 11
orangutan, 20

paleoneurology, 58
paleontology: artistic interpretation, 43, 50 *50,* 58; casts (*see* casts, plaster); comparative studies, 11, 18, 20, 25, 37, 44; field techniques, 14; fossil dating, 26–31; importance of Lucy, 18, 21, 56; muscle marks, 45; new techniques, 58; scientific method, 24
potassium, 29–30, *30*

stratigraphic column, 16, 26, *27, 28,* 29–31, *31*

Taieb, Maurice, *11*
Taung Child, 19, *19*
tool use, 32, 40, 54

walking: and bone structure, 37; and brain size, *21, 32;* as a hominid characteristic, 9, 56; Lucy, 10, 21, 32–42, *38;* theories on origin, 40–41
Walter, Bob, *28*

x-ray, *33,* 37

Zinj, 19, *19*

For Jim Ryan, whose green pen and 36Cs and 17Bs caused me much misery in high school—and helped me become a better writer in the process. Teachers make a difference. And I thank you.

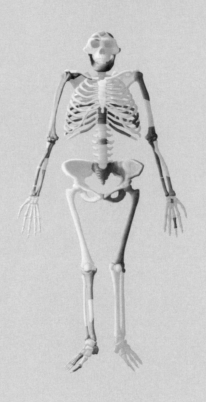

Houghton Mifflin Books for Children is an imprint of Houghton Mifflin Harcourt Publishing Company.

www.hmhbooks.com

The text of this book is set in Myriad Pro.

Library of Congress Cataloging-in-Publication Number 2008036761
ISBN-13: 978-0-547-05199-4

Printed in China
WKT 10 9 8 7 6 5 4 3 2 1